Now Let's Make Some Adjustments and Walk in

Our Divine Royalty!

Are you ready? This supplemental workbook has been created so that we not only talk about our divine royalty, but it gives us the opportunity to WALK IN IT! These tips, lessons, and suggestions have been a blessing to my walk. So I wanted to share and bless you with them as the Holy Spirit has blessed me. The goal is to help move you beyond your potential and into your greatness. Greatness is what you possess, but you have to know and believe it so that it will activate and show up in your life. Consistently apply these tips to your everyday way of life and watch your life change by GOD's grace! It takes daily action and intentional change to see the difference. Again I ask... ARE YOU READY?

Crowned

Get To Know GOD...

For Real!

Date GOD and yourself! HE will show you just how special you are and how you're to be treated and loved not only by your future spouse but in every relationship. Start building a true relationship with HIM. Nothing or no one should come before GOD in your life. Get close to HIM so that you will know and have certainty about who you are according to HIS word and what HE says about you! As well as the call and purpose HE has for your life. It is of the most importance that you seek GOD diligently to reveal your purpose to you. When you are aware of your true purpose and/or purposes when you meet "the one", it will be easier to identify your purpose together as partners. Complete fulfillment in life shows up through our GOD-given purpose.

Ask yourself what does it mean to have a true relationship with GOD? What exactly does that look like to you? Explain...

_____

_____

_____

Is prayer important to you? Do you have an active prayer life? What does that look like for you? Forget the formalities...do you talk to GOD? Answer below...

_____

_____

_____

Seeking GOD for your purpose is so specific to your journey. If you are uncertain of your purpose, that's ok; however, you should take the time to diligently seek GOD for that answer. The scriptures of HIS Word are a great place to start. Do you Study the Bible for your own understanding? Who from the Bible or a combination of can you relate to and why? Write it out below...

Do you outwardly honor GOD with praise and worship? Praise and worship show honor and reverence for our Heavenly Father. It also presents a humble character trait that all believers should carry. When expressed from the heart, praise and worship can feel like pure love to your spirit from GOD's Holy Spirit. How do you feel about praise and worship? Explain below...

Are you willing, or do you ever have an evening out alone? While really enjoying your own company? What do you like to do and where do you go? When I say date GOD and yourself, that's exactly what I mean. So...do you?

Forgive...Apologize...Never Pass *Judgment!*

Forgive or apologize and stop passing judgment! I didn't say don't forget, but you should forgive and move on. Even if that takes a while, forgive because no one person is perfect, including you. GOD has forgiven all of us time and time again. That also means we should drop the pride, be accountable for our actions, and apologize when needed. A King or Queen will always take the high road and be the bigger person. You're royalty, right? Last but not least, never pass judgment. You don't have it all figured out, nor do you live a perfect life, so who are you to judge...ijs. If you are perfect, then, by all means, carry on.

Do you have a problem with forgiving others when they hurt or offend you? Be honest with yourself; if not, it's ok; it's definitely a process. I used to be the biggest grudge holder alive...no lie. Did you know that as a member of the Kingdom of GOD you are obligated to forgive? Write about your experience in this part of your walk!

_____

_____

_____

_____

_____

_____

_____

_____

How about owning your part or mistakes
and apologizing? This can be an extremely
tough one...

Do You find yourself being really
judgemental of others or their actions? I
catch myself daily and remind myself that
whatever "they" got going on is none of my
business. That's how I stay in my lane! What
about you? Honestly ask yourself if you're
the judgy type. Talk about it below...

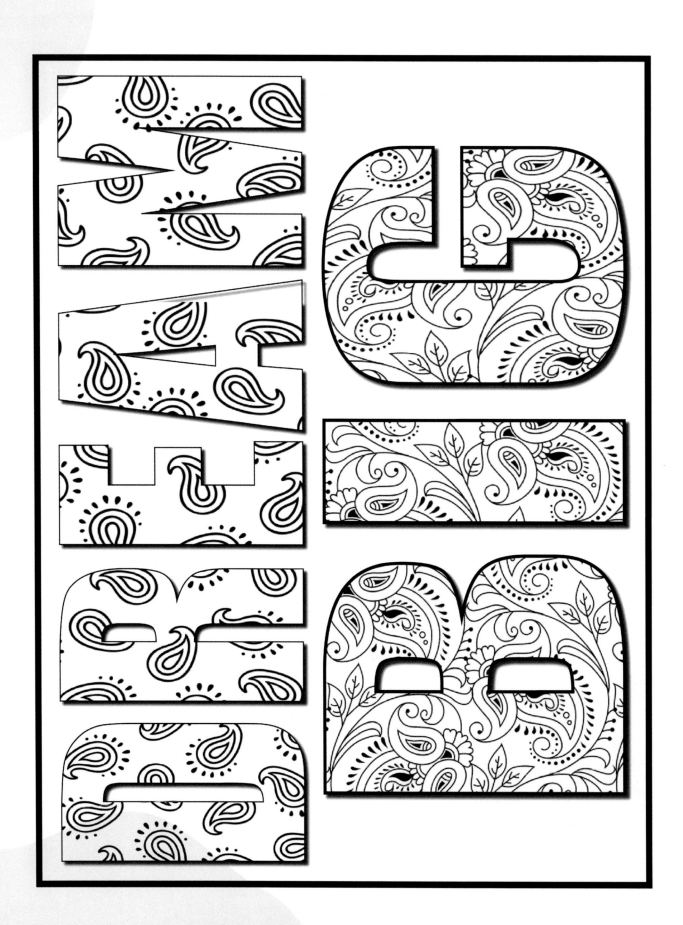

Speak To Her...

She's Listening!

Affirm and confirm who you are, who you are, and what you want to accomplish every day. Literally say it out loud to yourself! Nobody has the power to encourage you and push you like YOU do. Please converse with the Queen in the mirror on a daily basis. She's counting on you. No one knows her like you do or has the ability to LOVE her like you do. Are you willing to show up for the Queen in the mirror?

Do you believe you can speak things into existence according to the Word of Almighty GOD? Ezekiel 12:25

_____

_____

_____

_____

_____

_____

_____

_____

You should have a daily affirmation routine that you speak out loud, consistently. Write down some things that GOD your Heavenly Father says about you HIS precious daughter. Let's Goooooo...here's a few examples to get you started!

I Decree and Declare...

I am Saved by The Blood.

I am Fearfully and Wonderfully Made.

I am Protected.

I am Loved.

I am cont'd...Fill up these pages with all the beautiful things GOD says about you!

Embrace

Change is inevitable and necessary for growth. Does it feel good? Most times, it doesn't. We must let go and just roll with whatever steps HE orders for us, and I agree that can be a bit of a challenge. However, don't overthink it, and don't concern yourself with how, why, when, what, or who. Just go with GOD's flow and enjoy the scenery. No, seriously, the process or road can be really tough at times but KEEP GOING! While you're at it, take some time to look around and soak it all in...you'll thank me later.

In your past, have you struggled with accepting change? For most people, change is naturally hard. It's ok if this has been a challenge in your life. We're doing the work now to fix that! So be honest...

_____

_____

_____

_____

_____

_____

_____

So we know that living in this world, change is going to happen. It's just the natural cycle of life, right? Let me ask you this, though...are you willing to change to grow into the best version of you? If you are, then tell me what some of those changes look like for you.

Are you ok with giving some of it (life's craziness) over to GOD and resting in HIM? This is a really big question, so don't answer too quickly. People will say yes and be telling a flat-out lie. Guess what, though, if you're not quite ready for that kind of Faith release, it's totally fine because HE loves us enough to wait on us. Are you ready to release...yes or no? Why or why not?

I'm not going to sugarcoat this one, and it honestly takes a level of maturity to even be able to embrace what I'm about to ask. When you're in the middle of one of life's tough storms...are you open to embracing the process? GOD's Word says to count it all joy, but be honest with yourself. Are you kicking and screaming the entire time, or are you asking for the lesson to be revealed in the midst of the struggle? How do you handle the pressure? Do you let it get the best of you, or do you patiently (as possible) wait out the storm? Explain...

HE Doesn't Need Us...

We need him.

Don't make things that don't matter so much...matter too much. Don't sweat the small stuff, and stop concerning yourself with the wrong things. Breathe, let go and let GOD. HE doesn't need your help.

Yep...Just like that! Half of the things that try to take up space in your mind are none of your business. Do you find yourself giving way too much energy to situations and people that really don't deserve it? Be honest...

_____

_____

_____

_____

_____

_____

_____

We worry about the wrong things. We've all done this, and again, this is where maturity kicks in. When you stop concerning yourself with what others think and little minor things that are totally irrelevant, you find yourself in a much more peaceful space. Don't let insecurities drive your peace away. How often do you get consumed by the small stuff? Why or why not?

GOD doesn't need our help...shocker, I know! We women can be synonymous with trying to fix something, some situation, or someone. No, not you...well, definitely me in the past. I've learned to pray about it, whatever it is, and forget about it. GOD doesn't need my help or yours. Give some examples of when you tried to fix it. As well as a time when you took your hands off of it, and HE fixed it.

Search:

How Do You
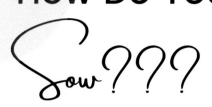

Sow???

You will not grow if you do not sow. Just like seeds that we plant for flowers and food, well, if we didn't plant the seeds, we wouldn't get the flowers or the food, right? How and what are you sowing back into the earth and Kingdom? Be it love, energy, time, sweet words, or money, SOW something, Queen! Let me ask you this, why did you wake up this morning? If not to improve this world, then why? Do something for someone else and watch how it will enrich and bless your life.

How do you give/sow into your local community?

_____

_____

_____

_____

_____

_____

Would you be open to giving/sowing on a larger scale? Like doing a mission trip abroad?

Do you sow/give from your heart or out of obligation? Why or why not?

What's one of your favorite ways to give back or sow?

Intentionally Live Your

Best life!

Vacation! Travel! Be Adventurous! Go somewhere you've never been, whether here or abroad, just go! Do something you've never done! Go for a hike in the mountains of Denver, CO, or a bike ride on Creeper Trail in VA. Go skiing in Aspen, go for a swim in the Atlantic Ocean...just go! Apply for your passport and start saving! Start working out consistently, or join a boxing club; just take the limits off! Go and see all the beauty GOD has blessed us with on this earth. Venture into new lands, meet new people, and experience new things and new cuisine. Be open-minded when you go; you never know what you will experience on your adventure! GOD has some amazing blessings waiting for you out there!

> Are you open to new adventures? If so, list 5 things that you would be open to do here in the US?

_____

_____

_____

_____

_____

_____

Have you ever traveled outside of the country? If so, where have you gone, and where would you like to go next?

Waiting on others to participate can oftentimes slow you down or hinder you from going altogether. Are you open to traveling by yourself? Why or why not?

Did you know that traveling and being open to new experiences adds to your legacy? What kind of legacy do you want to leave behind?

What or where is the most beautiful place you've laid your eyes on? Why?
Ex. NYC skyline...

NEW CREATURE

Praise HIS
Mighty name!

Praise HIS Mighty Name!
At all times, and I do mean AT ALL TIMES... give HIM all the honor, glory, praise, and credit! We can't BE without HIM. Why would we want to? It's that simple.

> Stop and think for 60 seconds about how you truly feel in your heart about GOD.
> Write down what you felt in your heart...

_____

_____

_____

_____

_____

_____

_____

Write 5 or more personal experiences where GOD protected and kept you...

It's that Simple.

Always wear your crown...but help another Queen with hers too! In Matt. 22:39 GOD tells us clearly in HIS Word..."Love your neighbor as yourself." To me, this is the answer to world peace! We should be walking examples and doers of Love to one another. I'm only as strong as my fellow sister or brother...

How do you personally show up for others daily? Give a few examples...

Do you have a heart for others, or are you a bit self-centered? Do you want to change; why or why not?

Do you need help loving yourself first? Be honest, it's totally ok if you do. Are you willing to work on this area of your life with intention?

GOD IS LOVE...

Walk in HIS Love...always.
Pure, genuine, honest, and sweet!
Walk in HIS Love...always.

- Briyia

Words To Live By

C	E	N	G	C	B	E	A	U	T	I	F	U	L
R	R	M	E	R	N	D	E	W	R	G	S	S	N
O	E	M	I	T	E	V	E	T	I	N	L	O	R
W	E	E	U	R	I	G	L	T	O	S	I	P	E
N	S	T	A	T	R	O	G	I	F	T	D	R	E
E	O	P	A	R	V	O	T	I	A	I	A	O	E
D	P	E	R	E	O	A	R	E	D	C	G	V	M
F	R	R	D	Q	M	Y	R	G	F	L	E	U	R
C	U	F	M	R	U	C	A	L	R	I	A	E	A
D	P	D	I	F	W	E	E	L	L	O	Q	O	L
A	D	F	E	E	E	S	E	E	T	E	W	I	G
M	F	D	N	N	E	E	B	N	A	Y	W	T	O
A	G	R	E	F	L	E	C	T	I	O	N	R	H
N	E	M	P	O	W	E	R	E	D	G	E	R	E

CROWNED
AFFIRMATIONS
GROWTH
ROYALTY
GOAL DIGGER
EMPOWERED
BELIEVE
CREATIVE
REFLECTION
BEAUTIFUL
SELF CARE
QUEEN
TIME
PURPOSE
LOVED
GIFTED
NEW CREATION
WISDOM
MIRROR

Last but actually first, always lead with love. It will take you so very far, further than you could possibly imagine. GOD loved us first... 1 John 4:19, and HE is Love.

What does HIS Love mean to you?

Hi Kings and Queens ...

I pray your life was blessed and enriched by the pages of this book. On that note I must give all the credit, praise, and honor to our heavenly Father for allowing me to be the vessel to bring forth this word. My prayer is that lives will be transformed from this project. That men, women, and young people will begin to walk in their divine royalty. Life transformation starts with salvation through Christ Jesus. So right where you are, no matter your age, social class or status, race, gender, situation, or circumstances, you can give your life to GOD today! Simply say this short but sweet prayer out loud and declare Jesus as your Lord and Savior! HE is waiting just for you.

- Briyia

Dear Heavenly Father,

I thank you that as I come to you, you will in no way cast me out. I thank you that you did not send Jesus into the world to condemn it but that the world might be saved by Him. I am your child because I believe that your son Jesus died on the cross for my sins and was raised from the dead on the third day. I decree and declare that He is my Lord and Savior and that I am washed and cleansed by His blood. I confess my sins to you now. I thank you that you are faithful to forgive me and to cleanse me from all unrighteousness. I thank you for I am now in right standing with you.

In Jesus Name ... Amen

–1John 1:9; John 3:16

I AM LIVIN' THIS QUEEN LIFE

About
the Author

Sobriyia Rucker, also known as Big Mama and the Bling Queen was born and raised in Dayton, OH, and is currently a resident of Charlotte, NC. Sobriyia's passion for GOD's people is what drives her. A natural giver, she loves to encourage others to be their best and give their best in every situation. A philanthropist and advocate of teens and young adults, she loves to help them excel and see their greatness.

As a Kingdom serial entrepreneur, the owner and operator of Big Mama's Sauce LLC, and Bria's Bling, respectively. Both web-based businesses are currently run from Charlotte, NC. She started Bria's Bling in 2012 on Faith with the number one goal of glorifying GOD through the business since HE released the vision for it to her. Big Mama's Sauce LLC came into complete existence in September of 2019. Although she had been making the recipe for years for friends and family, she did not launch publicly until August of that year. She has an extraordinary following, not to mention love and support across the country. Ohio, Kentucky, and Tennessee, to name a few. North Carolina, and South Carolina, Texas as well as Alabama, and Mississippi and is continually growing. GOD is expanding her territory day by day. In May of 2017, she was graced by GOD to give away the inaugural Bria's Bling college scholarship.

Many call her mom, but the 3.5 that get the most hugs and kisses are Jermaine Jr., Kevin, and JaBria. Rocco, the fur baby of the family, is a mini dachshund but thinks he's a pitbull.

Connect with the Queen..

🌐

www.livinthisqueenlife.com

✉️

livinthisqueenlife@gmail.com

📷

@livinthisqueenlife

Made in the USA
Middletown, DE
07 February 2024

49224595R00020